Unlearning to Draw

Received on:

MAY 0 9 2015

Green Lake Librar

NO LONGER PROPERTY OF
SEATTLE PUBLIC LIBRARY

D0448633

LEARNING TO SEE

If you've ever wanted to learn
to draw, or to draw better,
the Learning to See series offers
a mix of inspiration, encouragement,
and easy-to-complete exercises
that will have you filling the
pages of your sketchbook more
confidently in short order.

Unlearning to Draw

Peter Jenny

Princeton Architectural Press · New York

For Jack

Published by
Princeton Architectural Press
37 East Seventh Street
New York, New York 10003

Visit our website at www.papress.com

Originally published by Verlag Hermann
Schmidt Mainz under the title *Anleitung
zum falsch Zeichnen* © 2003 Die Professur
für Bildnerisches Gestalten, Professor
Peter Jenny, ETH Hönggerberg, Zurich
and Verlag Hermann Schmidt Mainz.
The text of the English edition has been
adapted to the American market.
English edition
© 2015 Princeton Architectural Press
All rights reserved
Printed and bound in China
18 17 16 15 4 3 2 1 First edition

No part of this book may be used or
reproduced in any manner without written
permission from the publisher, except in
the context of reviews.

Every reasonable attempt has been made
to identify owners of copyright. Errors or
omissions will be corrected in subsequent
editions.

For Verlag Hermann Schmidt Mainz:
Design: David Schlatter
Assistants: Aline Telek, David Schlatter,
Reto Spillmann

For Princeton Architectural Press:
Editor: Nicola Brower
Translator: Bronwen Saunders
Typesetting: Jan Haux

Special thanks to: Meredith Baber,
Sara Bader, Janet Behning, Erin Cain,
Megan Carey, Carina Cha,
Andrea Chlad, Tom Cho, Barbara Darko,
Benjamin English, Russell Fernandez,
Will Foster, Jan Cigliano Hartman,
Mia Johnson, Diane Levinson,
Jennifer Lippert, Katharine Myers,
Jaime Nelson, Rob Shaeffer, Sara Stemen,
Marielle Suba, Kaymar Thomas,
Paul Wagner, Joseph Weston,
and Janet Wong of
Princeton Architectural Press
—Kevin C. Lippert, publisher

Image credits:
Pages 100–1: Anni Brühweiler
Pages 120 and 154: Urs Lüthi

Library of Congress
Cataloging-in-Publication Data

Jenny, Peter, 1942–
[Anleitung zum falsch Zeichnen. English]
Unlearning to draw / Peter Jenny.
    pages cm
ISBN 978-1-61689-373-6 (paperback)
1. Drawing—Technique. I. Title.
NC730.J45813 2015
741.2—dc23

2014045945

Foreword

Unlearning to draw? Ignoring perspective? Scrawling, scratching, scribbling? Refusing to differentiate between a "right" and "wrong" way to draw is likely to provoke consternation and raised eyebrows, but refusing to fulfill expectations is precisely the point here, since raised eyebrows generally signify a readiness to ask questions. Most adults at some point give up drawing in the belief that they have no talent for it. Persuading you to take it up again, to relearn how to think visually, requires not just encouragement, but some hands-on tricks of the trade as well. One such trick is to develop an egocentric gaze. Children's drawings are a good example of this, as is the work of outsider artists, whose works do not conform to expectations; their scrawlings and doodlings may not have any intrinsic meaning, but they do at least deter us from making all-too-hasty judgments.

Drawings are clues that help us understand and appropriate the world we inhabit.

Before you begin sketching, you first need source material for your drawings. Private snapshots are ideal for this purpose and will help get you started. Photos like the ones used for this book can be found in pretty much every family photo album. Looking at other people's private pictures may make you uneasy, since none of us feels comfortable in the role of voyeur. I would like to apologize for inflicting this on you in this book. Since private motivation is essential to enjoyment, you will naturally have to work with your own photographs. Those who would prefer to leave the theory until later can start drawing at once by skipping to page 21.

Peter Jenny

Introduction

How outsider artists helped me see

I wouldn't dream of expecting you to understand the pictures of the mentally ill right away. But if the famous Swiss painter Paul Klee found inspiration there, you can be sure there's more to such works than meets the eye.

Those who regard pictures drawn or painted by the mentally ill as a lesson in how to see are bound to end up rethinking all their previous value judgments. The German psychiatrist and art historian Hans Prinzhorn collected thousands of such drawings and paintings between 1919 and 1921, and the book he published on the subject, *Artistry of the Mentally Ill*, was highly influential on the art scene of the time, including Jean Dubuffet who would coin the term *Art Brut* to describe works produced by people working outside aesthetic norms. Locked up, isolated, neglected, and deprived of any proper care or meaningful occupation, countless patients in psychiatric institutions found art to be their only outlet for venting their illness and lending shape to their fears. Driven by their own inner logic and distress, they communicated by sculpting and crafting, and by painting and drawing on what-ever came to hand, be it packing paper, news-print, or wood. While Prinzhorn avoided using the term *art* to describe their creations, the Austrian psychiatrist Leo Navratil, who, in the late 1950s, encouraged his patients at the Viennese Maria Gugging Psychiatric Clinic to produce drawings, had no such qualms and used the word *art* as a matter of course. Some of his patients would become known as the Gugging

Artists. Navratil's verdict makes sense, at least when considered against the backdrop of World War II; since it would be presumptuous of me to draw conclusions of a medical nature, I shall confine myself here to a discussion of the question of form. The works of artists such as Paul Klee, Louis Soutter, and Le Corbusier, and in our own day of German artists Hanne Darboven and Rosemarie Trockel and Japanese conceptual artist On Kawara, recall the exhibits in the Prinzhorn Collection, the output of the Gugging Psychiatric Clinic, and the Collection de L'Art Brut in Lausanne, France. In exceptional cases, art therapy for the mentally ill has indeed brought forth works that have a lot of overlaps with art. The qualifier "exceptional cases" is not intended pejoratively here; after all, art is always the exception, even among artists. More than a few artists, moreover, have learned from the unconventional aesthetic of those whom society tends to marginalize.

This little book is not about creating works of art, however, so the point of the exercise has to be sought elsewhere. Not only will we become acquainted with unconventional ways of seeing and learn how to relate these to ourselves and to the world we inhabit, but we will also discover the kind of perception that can eventually contribute to the creation of cultural commodities of our own. It is to achieve this that you will need to make a museum of your own—an art gallery hung with pictures drawn or painted by you that will enable you to develop ways of seeing that are not premised on conformity. The outsider artists who helped me see say, draw, and write what they mean and not what they do not mean. Their feelings are so strong that there is simply no space for sacrificing self-expression to good manners. Some of them are considered great artists who prefer not to be put to the test; as people who are mentally disturbed they have enough trouble as it is, without having to discuss the principles underlying their unique way of seeing. And these are the ones we want to learn from; their will to create will inspire us to create pictures of our own.

Homegrown culture

Family photos tend to be schematic in their composition and content. This is nothing you should worry about, however, because even a mediocre snapshot can contain the seeds of something that is anything but mediocre.

Everything that surrounds us, shapes us, and preoccupies us in the long term, is culture. The radius within which we "cultivate"—driven by gut instinct or calculation—is scarcely larger than the one that nourishes our perception and our powers of imagination. The metaphor of the global village usurps the value of personal experience only for as long as the average newscast lasts. No matter how far afield it may roam, culture thrives best close to its own headwaters.

We all take photographs and are photographed
and hence are contributing to a gigantic produc-
tion line of images that, once archived in the
family album, is unlikely to escape our own four
walls. The family album is the quintessential
bestseller, and as one family album looks much
like another it could be said that we are all
contributing to a publication that it is beyond our
capacity to imagine. Yet for all their similarities,
the pictures in this publication were shaped by
personal thoughts, personal joys and sorrows,
and personal relationships. This enormous stock
of schematic images in fact allows us to maximize
the individuality of our personal perception.
Fleeting moments forever frozen in time show us
what we once deemed worthy of a picture, and
what we would like to remember. The reason for
the photo or the circumstances in which it
was taken may be utterly banal. (Other people's
family albums are bound to bore us, just as
ours will undoubtedly seem tedious to them.)
Contemplating these fragments of memory

changes the way we feel about life. Visual ideas spring to mind against the backdrop of our own private province, and it is these transferable images that form the provincial culture to which we most truly belong. The act of looking fires the imagination, kindling new images that give us an inkling of our cultural roots. Viewing the familiar pictures from a slightly different angle and thus defamiliarizing them lets us see their content with new eyes.

Defamiliarizing the familiar

When we blink, what changes is not the distant but the nearby. Television would have us stop blinking altogether, encouraging us to rely on someone else's view of the world; but when you take a closer look at your own photos, you will continue to form your own pictures.

The photos in our family albums are so familiar that they are easy to overlook, unless we make a determined effort to study them in depth. There are many different ways of doing this: You can mentally reconstruct the occasion on which the picture was taken; you can copy the photos and select a new frame (on a photocopier or the computer); you can extract certain elements and rearrange them to create new images (whether in Photoshop or using scissors and paste); or you can take a pen or pencil and draw all over them. Whichever method you choose, you will gain ways of seeing that take you beyond the standard view through the camera's viewfinder or that provided by your photo album. Your mind will go back and forth between ideas and notions elicited through viewing the pictures in a new light and the materialization of a new image.

Defamiliarization is an integral aspect of every act of viewing, if only because of the collision of past and present, and provides the ideal starting point for lending the familiar strangeness surrounding you a new visual idiom. To preclude any misunderstandings: As much as we want to learn from the artists at the Gugging

Psychiatric Clinic, there are no hidden therapeutic intentions here; our sole concern is to derive new insights.

My intention in urging you to defamiliarize the familiar is by no means trivial, for the goal consists in nothing less than the discovery of a hitherto unknown visual culture within your own four walls. To achieve this goal, however, you must redefine the relationship between "normal" family photos and "abnormal" reworked photos. The question of what is normal or abnormal always depends on the prevailing conventions and consequently does not transfer well. One man's trash is another man's treasure; what makes sense to one is nonsense to another. But when it comes to our own visual habits it can only broaden our horizons if we learn from people who think differently, who are bound by their own conventions and obsessive about abiding by them. Try and see the pictures produced by the inpatients at the Gugging Psychiatric Clinic and other outsider artists as an encouragement to create your own family museum. You could call the picture gallery of your museum your "Album Brut," a name derived from Art Brut, or outsider art, which is more about discovery than about artistry.

If you could arrange your photo album any way you wanted, unshackled by convention, then probably all the great themes of everyday life would come to the fore: love, sexuality, sickness, death, children, festivities, work, money, personal endeavor. The more appealing the images are, the more dazzling their colors, and the happier the faces, the stronger is the will to change our view of things. What counts is not the colors or the highlights, but your love and longing—the great themes of art, in other words. Should you succeed in making "art," then it will be thanks only to yourself and in spite of this little book. It is perfectly sufficent to make pictures that show who you are.

Exercises in Dexterity and Perception for an Unorthodox Start

Pages 22 to 63 are full of ideas that you can try out for yourself. The examples invite abuse, free interpretation, and the defacement of drawings on the printed page (to use the book itself as a sketchbook). Playfulness is much more important here than following examples to the letter. The thematic exercises begin on page 64.

Ready... Steady... Draw!

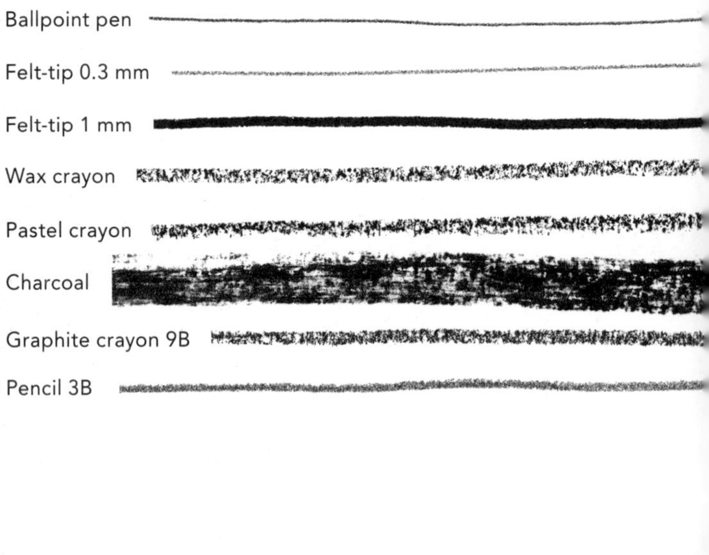

Ballpoint pen

Felt-tip 0.3 mm

Felt-tip 1 mm

Wax crayon

Pastel crayon

Charcoal

Graphite crayon 9B

Pencil 3B

Exercises in dexterity and perception: types of line

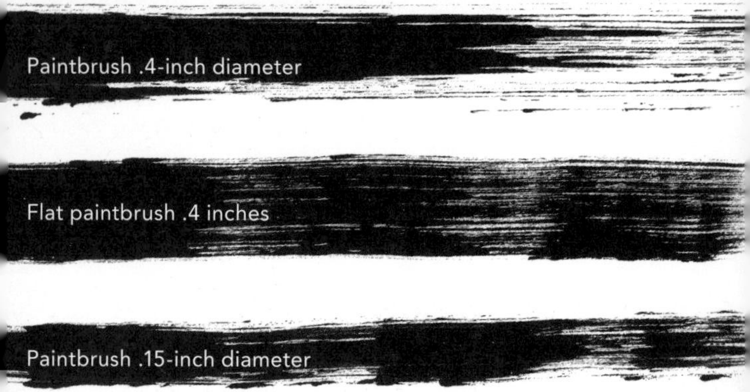

Paintbrush .4-inch diameter

Flat paintbrush .4 inches

Paintbrush .15-inch diameter

Undiluted acrylic paint

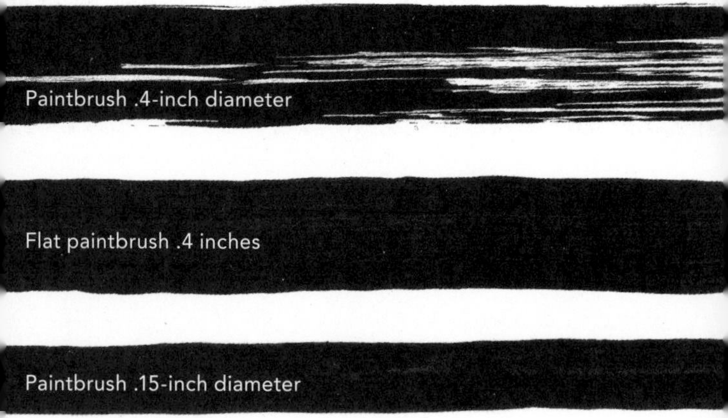

Paintbrush .4-inch diameter

Flat paintbrush .4 inches

Paintbrush .15-inch diameter

Diluted acrylic paint

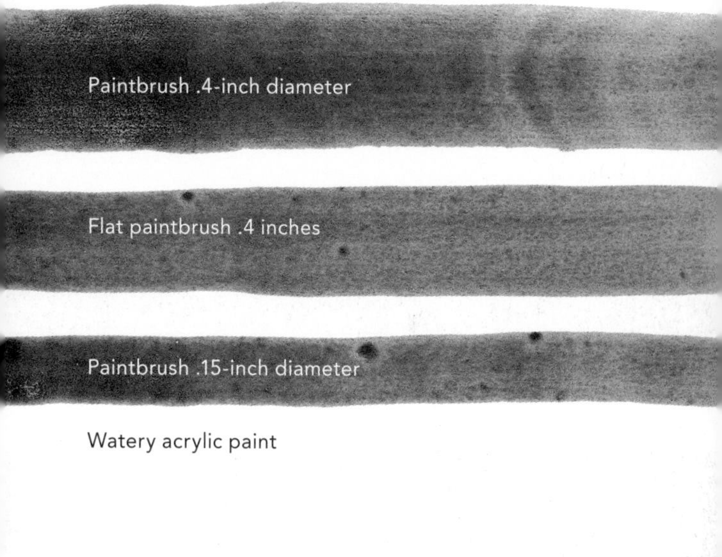

Paintbrush .4-inch diameter

Flat paintbrush .4 inches

Paintbrush .15-inch diameter

Watery acrylic paint

Color application

Frieze

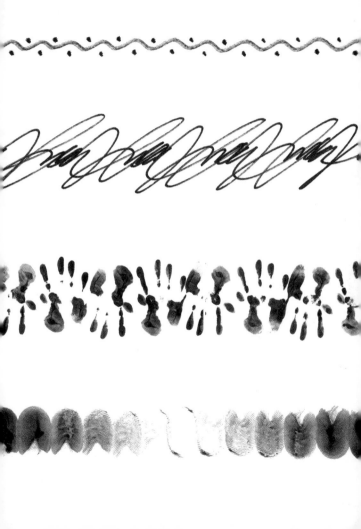

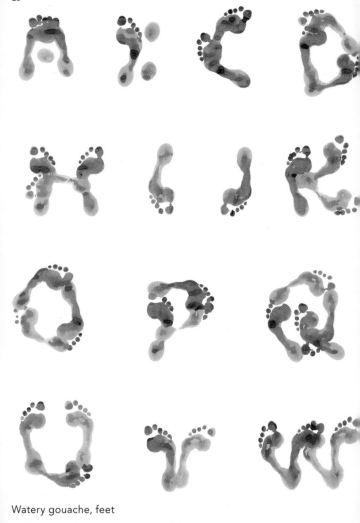

Watery gouache, feet

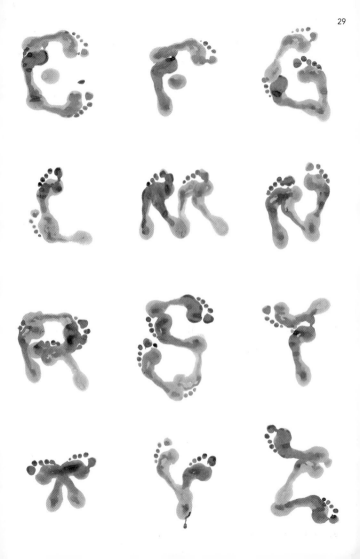

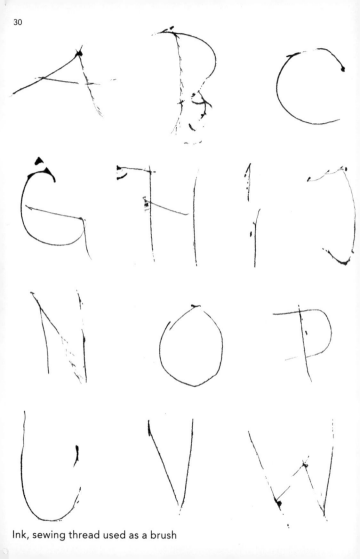

Ink, sewing thread used as a brush

Wax crayon, finger nails

Watery acrylic paint, fingers

Watercolor, watercolor brush

Ink, fingers

Acrylic paint, fingers

Acrylic paint, fingers

Undiluted acrylic paint, paintbrush .4-inch diameter

Diluted acrylic paint, paintbrush .4-inch diameter

Mirroring

Drawing after photos

Ornament

Caricature and drawing after photos

Playing with perspective

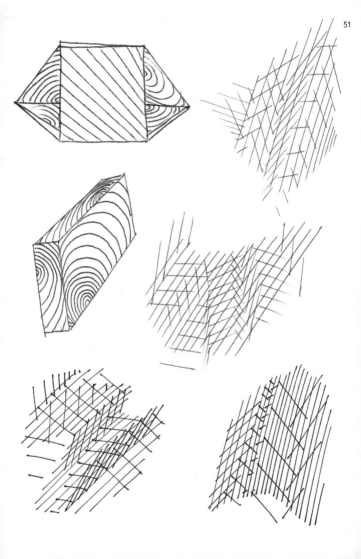

Grimaces and faces

Personification

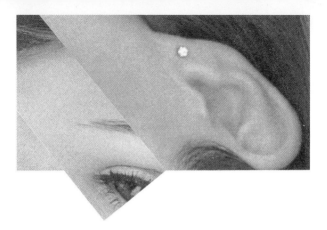

Collage

Charcoal

Modeling after photos

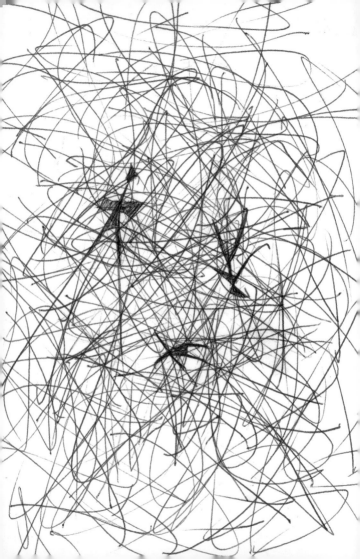

Searching

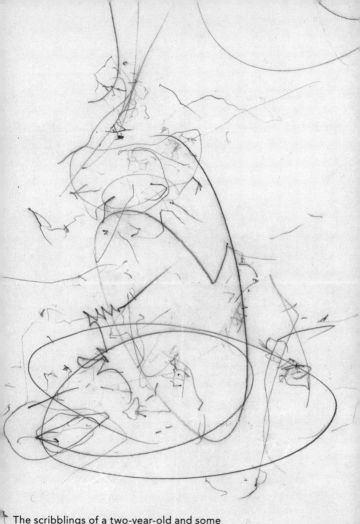

The scribblings of a two-year-old and some figures that an adult might see in them

1

The exercises on the
following pages are based
on your own personal
photos. The examples
provided here are meant
to serve as inspiration
for various forms of
interpretation through
drawing. Please refer to
pages 198 to 200 for a
selection of technical and
organizational options.

You and I

Strip familiar images of their personal meaning in order to develop new image-making techniques. Every private photo album is basically an accumulation of frozen instants, and the photos it contains are usually conventionally composed. Rediscover those views from a distance in order to turn snapshots into transferable impressions. Choose a photo of yourself with someone from your circle of friends and acquaintances and let your affections, recognizable hierarchies, desires, and longings influence how you present it.

2

I and We

Many of our photos show our parents, siblings, and friends. Much of what we know derives not from personal experience but from other fellow beings. Talking to others allows us not only to add to our own stock of experience but to reflect on it, too. Any statement that starts with "I" almost certainly also implies a "we." Our photos help us recall others, especially if we haven't seen them for a long time. In our case, however, the purpose of these photos is not only to conserve memories, but (possibly) to change them. For this exercise pick photos of your parents, friends, or of other people that have influenced you in some way.

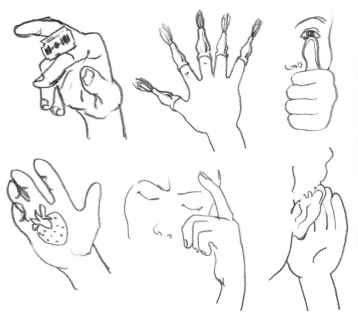

Further-reaching associations: fingers representing the five senses that grandfather keeps under his hat.

3

I and the World

The world is always circumscribed by the radius of personal experience. We can grasp only what we experience, for we are ultimately all regionalists. When we try to gain a larger perspective—whether of our immediate surroundings or a much larger area—we have to revert to a certain degree of abstraction. Since none of us can imagine the world in its entirety, we have to rely on abstract signs. The globe is but one example among many. Be inspired by your vacation snapshots to bring the world into your drawings.

4

Parts and the Whole

Shifting our view of things to other senses can make us more receptive to detail and complexity. "Feasting" with the eyes is a good example of such a shift. We can also attune our senses to how each neighborhood, each place in the world, has its own smells, its own sounds, and its own atmosphere. Our vacation photos from faraway locations pile up in our living rooms where they commingle with local views in a game of mix and match that invites weird and wonderful combinations. Make a drawing based on a photo taken in your intimate surroundings and then compare it to one inspired by a shot taken in a distant location. Or combine elements of both in one picture.

5

Same and Different

The objective of an individual is often at odds
with shared beliefs of how things should be. The
aesthetic governing family photos abides by
societal norms. While the results may hence be
similar, we can still apply different ways of seeing
to them, or we can play with these conventions.
Something can look different and have the same
content, or it can look the same and mean
something different. For the following exercise
choose or take pictures that follow the norms in
an unconventional way.

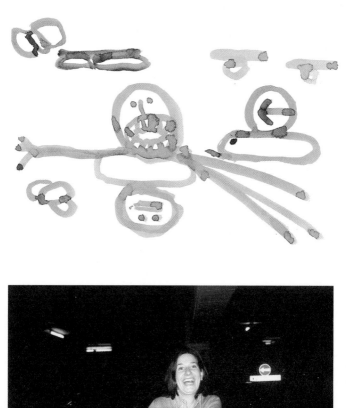

6

Object and Face

The act of drawing and discovering faces begins in childhood and can be linked with pleasure (laughing mouth) or with fear (grimace). Seeing faces everywhere fulfills two elementary functions: it is a means of making contact and it is a means of keeping disagreeable feelings at bay. Giving inanimate objects a face, as many children's books and comics do, is thus an archetypal urge. Anything and everything can be turned into a face. Children do it all the time; but so do adult artists and outsiders. Blurring can make the transformation easier. Imprecise images invite interpretation and lend themselves more readily to personification. Choose photos of inanimate objects and give them a face in your drawings.

How many faces can you see?

7

Life and Death

Images and language can stand in for actions or be experienced as actions. While life and death are categorical concepts, the terms *animate* and *inanimate* can be used instead and allow a rather less categorical interpretation. Through the use of images or language even an inanimate object can seem alive, just as a living organism can look dead. Play with this concept in your drawings.

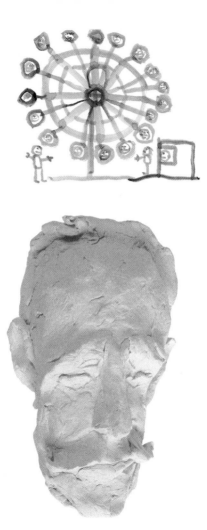

8

Static and Kinetic

The English photographer Eadweard Muybridge, in 1877, was the first man to make pictures move. In art, we may discover kinetic form in Cubist works by Georges Braque, Pablo Picasso, and Marcel Duchamp, among others—artists who drew inspiration from other cultures, other spheres of life, other sentiments. Cubism, understood as figures in motion, was also found in the pictures of the mentally ill. These artists borrowed from many sources and cared little for underlying causes; what interested them was what happened on the retina. Non-artists, too, can profit from this kind of nonchalance if they can muster some of the same readiness to engage in visual borrowings. For this exercise choose photos showing moving figures or objects and try out different ways to depict motion.

9

Inner and Outer

It is the inner gesticulation we want to capture, not the fumbling hands—to go from the visible to the imaginable, from effect to cause, from the words to the thought. These pairs of contrasts allow us to alter our ways of seeing in a wide range of ways. Analogies and contrasts between the aesthetic (perception) and the cosmetic (beautification) can lead to a wealth of themes for new pictures. Focus on the underlying emotions you can discover in your photographs of friends and family.

10

Emotional and Rational

Teasing new emotions out of old pictures by amplifying and distorting their content often provides a welcome opportunity to experiment with unexpected impressions and to break out of our "normal" patterns of perception. Whether it is anxiety you exaggerate in your drawings or joy, the amplification will lead to interesting results.

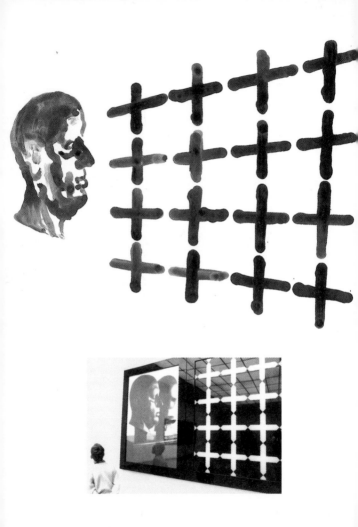

11

Paradox and Logic

A Fata Morgana may seem paradoxical but is perfectly logical in terms of both need and perception. Advertising works mainly with Photo Morganas—just think of images evoked by Coca-Cola or former Marlboro advertisements. Then there's the story of a woman who knitted giant socks whenever she had to spend any length of time in a psychiatric clinic. Paradoxical? Or logical? Desperate to escape, she invested all her time in knitting her own seven-league boots, which seems a lot more logical than the cigarette-smoking cowboy presented to us as a sales pitch. Yet it is the woman who counts as mad, not the smoker. Choose photos that may seem paradoxical at first glance and develop your own logic in drawings based on them.

12

Children's Drawings and Adults' Ambitions

Most people would like to draw the way others photograph. Their ineptitude may be great, but their obsession is greater still. Their art is a product of their obsessiveness alone, which forces them to come up with their own schemata. Overdrawing photographs with schematic forms can illustrate this point very well and contrast a child's way of drawing with an adult's ambition. Choose a photo to draw from and deliberately simplify its forms. Be inspired by your childhood drawings.

13

Wrong and Right

Perspective seems right. Photography seems right. That's the way things look, or so we believe. But what is right is also a question of adaptation. Perspective is an age-old method that attempts to take account of the delusory aspect of seeing. What we consider to be wrong or right has to do with societal norms. Wrong is supposedly the exception and right the rule. People who are mentally ill often feel a desperate need to express themselves and do so independently of notions of wrong or right. For your next drawing choose a photograph that shows yourself, family members, or friends in an exceptional circumstance. Take the "wrong" situation as an inspiration to experiment with form and content in your drawing.

14

Identification and Distance

We distance ourselves from excessive haste but identify with thinking ahead. The latter has a positive connotation because it is associated with the imagination. We can identify with something we know or have experienced and at the same time be forced to stand apart from it. To express both identification and distance in a picture, make the problem the subject rather than its solution.

15

Dream and Reality

Every image or thing can mean the opposite. The pictures we see when we dream are not real; they are irrational. The dreams of the supposedly "normal" people and the supposedly "abnormal" are perhaps very similar. Draw a picture that contains both real and dreamed-up aspects.

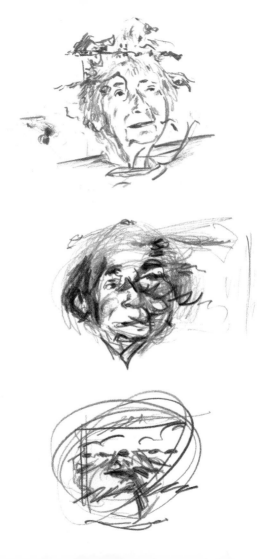

16

Image and Language

Language can lend a picture an extra dimension. Names can be associated with positive or negative images—just compare the connotation of names such as Kevin and Michael with that of Cain, Judas, or Adolf. To be called something is to be equated with reality; this explains why captions are so important, and why titles such as Dr., Prof., etc. matter to us. For this exercise use words to underline or transform the meaning of your picture.

Identity card Swiss citizen

Unsere Bilder sollen es einmal besser haben.

We want our images to be better off.

17

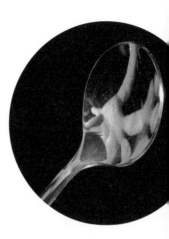

Portrait and Caricature

Caricature is not only about exaggeration or even defamation; it is also a way of poking fun. Caricature defies logic by tricking the viewer into abandoning all sense of proportion. Exaggeration gives viewers a chance to remind themselves of the rules; and exaggeration is fun: artists exaggerate; advertisers exaggerate; the mentally ill exaggerate. Draw a caricature based on a photographic portrait of someone you know well.

18

Value and Shifts in Value

To form a picture of something is to attach value to it. A shift in value is represented by mugshots or composite pictures. Different techniques are also associated with different values—a sketch is often valued less than an oil painting. Choose a photo of something or someone you value and try to either express this value or generate a shift of value in your drawing.

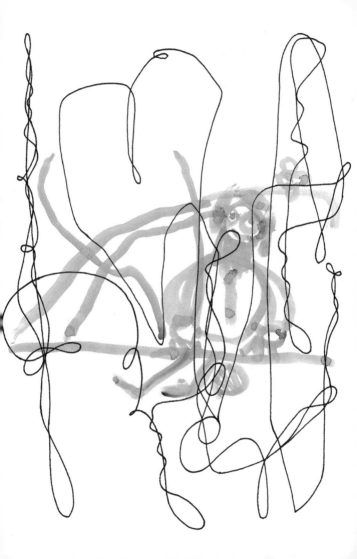

19

Repetition and Variation

No language can manage entirely without
repetitions and variations of the same thing.
In drawing, creating a pattern or a frame
performs much the same function. Such
repetitive forms of expression are used not just
in the visual arts and in language, but also in
music. Discover and repeat patterns in your
images. Make them the focus of your drawing.

20

Banality and Creativity

Every picture is the invention of an individual, even if it is based on many different sources. Depending on how it is used, an image can become banal or, by the same token (as in Pop Art), return to the realm of creativity. Banality versus creativity is a value judgment each of us makes when drawing or seeing something. For your next picture deliberately pick a photograph of a banal moment to spark your creativity.

21

Past and Future

When I speak of something that happened "four weeks ago," I am evoking images from my memory. When I say "in four weeks' time," I use my imagination. Only in pictures can past, present, and future be apprehended simultaneously. Perhaps the original purpose of the animals populating cave paintings was to ensure the success of the hunt. In your drawings try both to step back from effect to cause and at the same time to make the leap from effect to future consequence (a successful hunt).

22

Bashful and Brazen

Being bashful and coy used to count as a virtue in young women. This begs the question whether that made brazenness a virtue of mature women. Imitation counts as brazen in the visual arts, just as plagiarism does among writers. The drawings of the mentally ill often stand out precisely because of their brazenness. Be inspired by them and be brazen in your imitation of other artists.

Dies ist kein
Bild von
Ben Vautier!

René

"This is not a picture by Ben Vautier! René"
"Forge" a picture.

Select portraits from the annals of art history and take
pictures of yourself in the same poses.

The Album Brut

If there were such a thing as a secret academy for outsider artists, humor, hope, irony, invention, unreality, and untruth would have to be its themes for creation—subjects that you do not share with just anyone (which, incidentally, is another good reason for taking a closer look at them).

While Art Brut has to do with social relationships, the system and structures of psychiatric care, and of course the art business, the Album Brut remains in the realm of your own private picture gallery. This will make it simpler, though no less complex, and less ambitious while admitting of greater liberties, than would be possible if the rallying cry were "Warning! Art Ahead!" Creating your Album Brut will be complex and individual at the same time, because personal material of this kind does not lend itself readily to abstraction. While it will certainly draw from your network of relations, it will be focused only on extracts of your personal life and the content will thus remain manageable. Your toolbox will consist of your family album, your head, and your hands (even if you intend to work on the computer). You will be operating in a cultural milieu that you know well, but not well enough to rule out surprises, especially when people or things you know well begin to seem alien to you through defamiliarization. Better still, you will deal with people and pictures that are happy to join in because there are no copyright issues.

If we all regard our own vacation snaps as "true" to the extent that they provide a supposedly objective record of past events, then looking at them "askance" is a good way of giving your heart a jolt. At first glance, your pictures will tell us something about your ideal family, ideal vacation, ideal family relations, ideal weather. Yet it is precisely these "ideal" images that allow us to be self-critical. It is easy to use scissors or a pen to alter your own photos; and it is always easier to change yourself than it is to convert others (even if only to a different point of view), so feel free to be lazy for once, and instead of engaging in a futile struggle to convert your real family, content yourself with changing your own point of view. This will put you at the center of the action, even if you're not actually in the picture at all. Such altered family photos often attract comment and become a talking point. And there should be lots of talking in your family museum—as well as silence, cursing, and laughing, just like in any other museum. When I was young I was taught that good pictures speak for themselves, which is of course nonsense; for there can no more be pictures without words (the missing words being buried somewhere in our stock of experience) than there can be pictures that speak volumes. Pictures and words belong together. Both our perception and our nonverbal communication are informed by verbal knowledge.

Ah, only the retina!

Many critics nowadays seem to have adopted "the retina" as shorthand for an excessively superficial way of seeing. Of course, such criticism is never leveled at the blind. So next time prejudice gets in the way of your personal perception, try acting "blind."

When discussing my book project "Learning from Gugging" with a psychiatrist friend of mine, he naturally asked me what the working title was supposed to mean. I told him all about the famous book *Learning from Las Vegas* by a similarly famous pair of architects; this book deals with buildings that are premised on a way of thinking that is radically different from the early Bauhaus style, which was prevalent at the time. That unfamiliar way of thinking proved highly stimulating and arose out of a completely different set of values from those underlying early modernism. Different values and different concepts were brought to bear in the Gugging

Psychiatric Clinic, too. There, pictures took the place of medication (up to a point, of course) and personal expression took the place of sedation. This bore fruit in the form of pictures that can be categorized as Art Brut or outsider art. I also mentioned just how far our own perspective diverges from that of the "disturbed." When I was finished, my friend gently alerted me to the superficiality of reducing everything to the level of the retina and unabashedly reminded me of which fields can safely be left to perception researchers and designers and where the work of clinical psychiatrists begins.

He was right! Only he drew the wrong conclusions. Those who use the words "only the retina" dismissively are in fact exposing just how little they know about perception, since retina and brain are not so easy to separate. Putative norms can be questioned by replacing the usual with the unusual; I am, of course, aware that the simple fact that something comes "from the outside" does not provide it with meaning in itself. But by viewing these works we do at least discover a profound sense of freedom that is not defined solely by doing what seems right. If Paul Klee learned a lot from this kind of art, why shouldn't other people—by which I mean those outside the art business—profit from it, too? Appropriating another's behavior helps us master changes and rethink our own position. To do this, however, we have to let go of our prejudices, such as the idea that imagination and imitation are a contradiction in terms. Adjusting to the unfamiliar presupposes a delight in discovery.

The blind spots of your perception

Experts always claim to know best. If the training of artists was placed solely in their hands and "artist" was a protected academic title, we could scarcely expect any major changes. Develop your own ideas, on the other hand, and you will have something that is genuinely worthy of protection.

Schooling in perception should be a matter of concern not only for visual professions but for all of us. It is actually just as important as learning to read and write. As most schools neglect this discipline, however, most people have to teach themselves, which they do in a way that is likely to be haphazard and unstructured. Subculture, dilettantism, and Art Brut are not bound by any fixed notions of perception, yet they still deal with content that is of concern to us all. The mentally ill create pictures for their own personal use—pictures that are expressive of their own view of the world. The rewards are of a purely personal nature. Unlike their carers, the artists at the Gugging Psychiatric Clinic had no schooling, yet their carers still learned to learn from those in their care—an example I would like to follow. Specialization can deter people from following their own ideas; instead, they define themselves by adopting certain trends or wearing certain brands that show to whom they (would like to) belong and from whom they wish to set themselves apart. Those who elect not do this must expect not to be understood, as the language of trends and brands has become a global phenomenon, and expressions that do not conform to it are left behind. The family album offers a wealth of possibilities for creative design that does not depend solely on consumption and is closer to us than brand products. Its light promises to dispel the darkness of our own personal blind spots. Transforming and defamiliarizing the photos it contains are sure to yield something new—not just on paper but in your mind, too.

Freedom of interpretation

Try to glean from the photos in your album whatever you think might be beneficial for your ideas. Remember it is not the technique that should be new, only the way of seeing. And if the technique of your choosing helps you with this, then so much the better.

Maybe you bought yourself a new analogue camera just a few years ago and a short time later had to throw all that obsolete knowledge overboard (or stow it away in the hold of your memory) when the age of digital photography arrived. Whether analogue or digital, you have a choice of techniques here, since even obsolete technology can bring you closer to your goal. You're allowed to have anachronistic pastimes! Family chronicles age much faster than even technology: after all, every photo shows the past.

If you use your photos to help you with drawing, you will have no choice but to interpret them. You alone decide what is right or wrong; you alone decide what to focus on. Work with copies of your photographs rather than originals, so you can cut them up, draw on them, or otherwise "abuse" them.

Individual "ad hoc truths" are much more full of life than so-called "timeless" knowledge. Granted, knowledge derived from photos of Aunt Cynthia and Uncle Michael is not the kind of knowledge that will get you far careerwise; but it will have a knock-on effect in your private life, if it helps you develop new ways of seeing. You may remember some of your drawings as a child. If you can, try to reactivate those forms and silence your inner critic. You are doing this for yourself alone, so personal pleasure is more important than any kind of judgment.

Forming pictures

There are only a dozen different motifs in your family album? Don't worry, most art schools do not deal with more subjects.

Mum and Dad's golden wedding, Dana's confirmation, Uncle Oscar at the Biennale, Rachel and Meret at Christmas, and whatever other photo opportunities you have immortalized by snapping a picture—often it is a special event that has caused you to reach for the camera. The more basic moments of human co-existence often go underrepresented in the history of perception (if there were such a thing). The ancestral portrait galleries of Europe's noble houses read much like your family album, except that there the family members are captured in oil. Today photographs are so much a part of life that everything else has become special instead. Only when you find (invent?) a special way of seeing them can you make them exceptional again.

Believe in your own pictures

Self-confidence cannot be commanded, but it can certainly be encouraged. If no one else does it, try encouraging yourself. Self-confidence can be learned.

Do you ever doubt the truth of photos used in advertising? Do you sometimes doubt the artistic abilities of certain famous artists? Do you, every now and then, do the opposite of what your former teachers told you? Unless you answered "yes" to at least two of these questions, you are clearly a believer in authority.

Joking aside, however, yes/no questions rarely tell us anything about perception. What we practice most when it comes to perception is ignorance. We overlook, we fail to hear, we go off on a tangent, we forget—in short, we exercise a healthy degree of self-confidence. The term *ignorance* has negative overtones, but it is impossible to avoid given the sheer volume of impressions bearing down on us every moment of our lives. There are countless themes for creating images, some of which are more commonly appreciated than others because they allow both individuality and feelings of solidarity (for example the themes of the family museum). No one should believe that pictures arise solely through intuition. The need for expressing content is an important motif. Ignorance can give you the freedom to ask: What do I want? (Please note that we are talking here not about ignorance born of stupidity but about ignorance that generates scope.) Your family album reveals all sorts of needs—you only need to recognize them. This is the reason why I do not eschew writing instruction manuals and textbooks: I know that depending on who uses them, they will lead to completely different ways of seeing and hence to completely different pictures. The instructions they contain seek to broaden your perceptual horizons rather than teach new techniques. As I have mentioned in earlier publications, no one knows how perception in all its complexity really works (no more than we know what patterns define how we think).

I am constantly on the lookout for good reasons for these instructional books. A good reason might be that your life will be better if you are self-aware and if you, by creating pictures of yourself and others, whether serious or satirical, reflect on what makes you—and them—distinctive. The simplicity of your pictures can scarcely be measured by everyday standards, for they are a product of your affection. Your family museum should be inspired by similar motifs as those of early collectors of paintings and curiosities. They collected out of love, meaning that love as the criterion of ownership was always in the background. There is no shortage of pictures of expensive objects; but your own picture-worthiness is something you must fight for yourself.

The universe of the trivial

"Nothing in particular"—it is a pity that the most common situations are often woefully neglected by photographers. In fact, you need a very particular eye to discover "nothing in particular."

What many family albums lack are scenes of everyday life. Because cameras are seldom at hand when these occur and because minor moments of happiness simply go unnoticed: the play of light and shade in a puddle of oil; the surprising patterns of flattened chewing gum on the sidewalk; the crown of a tree silhouetted against the sky (in the shape of grandpa's head); a sunbeam glinting behind the open fridge door; a cloud that looks like the Matterhorn; the shape of a flying fish recognizable in a weathered wall; the hands of a little child playing happily with its own toes; ants gorging themselves on a smear of honey; Katsushika Hokusai's wave visible behind the porthole of a washing machine; a coil of orange peel; a cobweb caught in a window frame—all these motifs elude our interest because only rarely do our eyes register such tiny instants of happiness when they occur. The trivial things in life are like leaves floating past us on a stream; only when captured as a picture do they attract our notice; only then can we really grasp them.

Poorly taken photographs

Your own personal pile of photos is a mine for perceptual intervention. Poorly taken photographs especially are an invitation to do something with them.

"Failed" photographs—blurry, shaky, or underexposed shots, photos taken on the wrong type of film, in the wrong light, printed on wrong paper, showing the wrong frame—are often considered unwelcome or even forbidden in the art of photography. But when you begin looking at photos as raw material for further processing, you should develop the same kind of awareness as a cook who is both economical and inventive and strives to prepare meals without producing mounds of waste. The stacks of photographs are like a treasure trove of material that gives you a chance to slow down and look again. This calls for a second image-making process, a slow method that goes step by step, line by line, click by click. Out of the abundance in front of you, you can create collages, caricatures, and other transformations. Even the most absurd photos, perhaps especially, are an encouragement to try out new compositions. A selection that at first glance may look a little strange can lead to surprising results. The answer to the question of what appeals to us visually does not lie solely in the "successful shot." You alone decide whether the picture you make based on your photo(s) should be surreal, naturalistic, realistic, satirical, abstract, ironic, serious, witty, sad, loud, soft, ugly, or beautiful, and whether it should speak for itself or be combined with text. In the kitchen, too, the choice of dishes is dictated by the available ingredients—whether it is pancakes, tagliatelli, soup, pizza, or pie. The cuisine in many poorer countries is delicious even though, or perhaps because, it uses only the simplest ingredients. You have only to think of how even the most humble leftovers can be pleasing to both stomach and palate, and it is not hard to imagine how leftover images, as a resource rich in memories of love, friendship, and the legacy of time and family, might delight the eyes. Only in the course of time do we learn to appreciate these qualities and to understand how what had been tucked away in a drawer can be transformed into handmade treasures for our own use.

"I keep my eyes open"

True creativity cannot manage without copying. When we copy things we make mistakes. When we make mistakes we break rules in a way that casts doubt on the very same rules that we have broken. Develop a readiness to make mistakes and what you copy will lead to something new.

"I keep my eyes open," said Swiss ousider artist Alfred Leuzinger of Wattwil, when asked where his drawings came from. Words like *innovation, creativity, imagination,* and *inventive energy* were not part of his vocabulary. Yet his pictures populated by beetles, railways, and people are unique. "I keep my eyes open," he simply explained. Indeed, Leuzinger studied his motifs very carefully before committing them to paper. He believed that he only had to draw what he observed in order to produce an accurate illustration of the scene playing out in front of him. One of the most persistent fallacies that some people never tire of propagating is that imitation impedes creativity. In fact, the opposite is true. Whether visual or linguistic, imitation ranks among the most powerful incentives there are; it could almost be described as a fundamental human right. Yet to this day, imitation is derided as the pastime of those who lack inventiveness. Those famous artists who drew or painted after photos took care to destroy the photos as quickly as possible so as not to be labeled a mere copyist. (That this verdict has been applied rather less liberally since the second half of the last century is a most welcome development.) Working with photos from your own family album will prove helpful rather than harmful. Due to the high degree of reality they show, photos are likely to have a defining impact on perception. If all that you did was duplicate them, even if in a different medium, there would be little point to it. Your goal must be to develop a different way of seeing—essentially a new meaning, arrived at through a process of reduction.

Technical possibilities

The countless existing technical methods mean that we need to limit ourselves to a few. Technology is always just a means to an end. When too many means are needed to achieve the same end, clearly something has gone awry. This book encourages you to focus on four different methods, listed below.

1. Sketching with the aid of photos: reduce the gradations of brightness and produce a powerful pencil drawing with much starker contrasts.
2. Use charcoal to achieve simpler and more expansive forms.
3. Daub poster paint straight onto the paper with your fingers; this will change the expressiveness of the outcome all over again.
4. Photos lend themselves to modeling, too. The more you practice, the easier it becomes to leave the flat picture behind you and model small, fully fleshed-out sculptures.

Ordering possibilities

Not the police, but you alone are responsible for enforcing law and order in your collection of images. Be careful, though, because while keeping good order may count as a virtue, excessive orderliness soon degenerates into prissiness. Listed below are various methods for interpreting your photographs.

1. Drawing what you see on the photo.
2. Mirroring as a method of duplication that exposes the hierarchy implicit in a given picture.
3. Creating a frieze, which allows linear (left to right) repetition and represents a value judgment.
4. Making an ornamental pattern by "filling" a given area and then repeating and varying it, similar as in a frieze.
5. Personification as a way of lending inanimate objects a face (a car, a facade, a plant—almost anything can be furnished with a countenance).
6. Distorting perspective as a way of achieving "unnatural" juxtapositions and shifts in scale.

7. Making a caricature, which demands instant recognition of the most meaningful parts of a picture, which are amplified and overdrawn in a way that is neither offensive nor defamatory.

8. We arrange things with our hands; we prepare food with our hands; sometimes we even eat with our bare hands. So surely it is legitimate to draw with our bare fingers for a change.

Learning by doing

Learning by doing is not just an empty phrase. By making minor mistakes and developing a kind of "accent" you increase your awareness; accents can be beautiful—not just in language.

I have already explained why imitation is so fundamental to communication and mutual understanding. What may seem formulaic, superficial, and even false in theory, when actually applied proves that forms can be full of meaning. In art, as in science, learning by doing means conducting experiments. The parameters of scientific experiments are defined by the objective, those of artistic experiments by inclination, talent, and the artist's own private obsessions. In this little textbook I have tried to stake out a manageable number of possibilities for you to work with—as few as possible, as many as necessary. Restrictions vouch for quality. This is true not just of tools and techniques; even the greatest geniuses are talented only in certain areas. We would all like to be exceptionally talented, but let's be honest: Which of us can really master all the things we would like to? And why should we care about the talents of others? We should instead relish each new experiment of our own. Teaching and learning—both are in your hands and your hands alone.

Finite possibilities

More is less. Unlimited possibilities limit us—at least at first. In visual design, scarcity comes as a welcome opportunity to try out something new.

Any child who has ever held a crayon can tell you that there are countless techniques and tools. A child doesn't even need drawing paper, because the living room wall will do very nicely thank you, thus demonstrating the qualities of scarcity: almost anything can become an image carrier for those who lack paper. If I recommend restricting yourself, if I encourage you to imitate certain forms and not others, then only because restricting yourself is not the same as slavishly marching in step. To take the metaphor a stage further: If you can march you can run; if you can jump you can leap; if you can turn a corner you can trace a circle; if you can stamp your feet you can dance—and stumble. Reflect for a moment on how you learned to talk and think of all the many different ways in which you learned the language, eventually acquiring a command of it. A superfluity of toys thrust on a child is likely to do the opposite of what the parents intended. Their aim was probably to animate the child to play, not to thwart it. And imitation is always an essential part of finding our own voice. If you still feel ashamed when caught tracing, you should read that last sentence again and take it to heart.

The game of images that you play in order to stock your museum with a collection of its own is based on just a few technical and formal rules. In trying to teach you new forms of perception I have taken the liberty of "plagiarizing" certain Art Brut artists. They may count as "handicapped" when measured by society's norms, yet some of them are in fact shining examples of how to make a virtue of a necessity. It is as if their limitations had become their program for finding their own truths. Meaning is not a finished product to be lifted en bloc from images or texts; we all have to discover it for ourselves. If your school fails to teach you this, then you have to school yourself. And you'll find the alphabet you need for this among those who have scarcely spent any time in the classroom at all.

Making a virtue of necessity

There are some things that do not have to be learned by rote. When you sit down to draw, do it daily, but at your leisure; be dilettantish, but enjoy it.

When did you stop drawing? Probably at a point when you ratcheted up your expectations to such a level that drawing as a form of expression was crushed under the weight of them. Most amateurs turn to the skills of professional draftsmen for guidance, and even while admiring their craft fool themselves into thinking, "It's all there in my head; the problem lies in the execution." That's certainly possible. But the exact opposite is equally plausible, i.e. that your hands would be perfectly capable, if only your head knew what to do. So let's just forget this pointless division of head and hands and simply get down to doing what we want to do. If, for example, the standards by which you measure your own self-esteem prevent you from drawing experimentally, then do it in secret. Develop a secret passion; disengage from the value judgments that are inhibiting you; do whatever you find satisfying; do whatever you can do in secret; do whatever is not subject to the success imperative. And do it for as long as it takes to cook dinner—or at least spend as much time on it each day as you devote to brushing your teeth. Your need to invest more time in drawing pictures will develop of its own accord. The positive impact of self-satisfaction is something you must and will discover for yourself.

Let the wellspring of your imagination flow forth

Encountering your own pictures is like suddenly meeting old friends. You immediately notice certain changes, just as you would in someone you haven't seen for a while. In other words, you engage in comparative perception. Write down what you notice on a piece of paper.

Fortuna, Jupiter's firstborn once immortalized on the reverse of Roman coins, was originally a fertility goddess. There were temples to her all over Italy, and peasants came to these temples to pray for rain. Only in the course of time was her remit enlarged to include money, love, and health. The oldest link and its connection to water, however, is still the one I like best, because our imagination is like water. Imagination flows in abundance, knows no bounds, has no notion of normal or abnormal, and sometimes allows us to let go of reason altogether. Pictures (and fortunately not just pictures) enable us to translate imagination into knowledge—a kind of knowledge that is not for everyone, as it has to do with changing perceptions. Some may choose to ignore the stimuli lurking between the covers of their photo albums. But if you have read this far, then the sight of the sun setting over the Bay of Naples will make you think of more than just a smoldering red and ultramarine blue. Your family photos will trigger more than just memories. There will be happiness and goodwill too. And happiness and goodwill present a cornucopia of possibilities! That alone should be reason enough to get started.